Betsey Chessen • Samantha Berger

Scholastic Ltd

Design: Silver Editions

Photo Research: Silver Editions

Endnotes: Lisa Feitel

Endnote Illustrations: Anthony Carnabucia

Photographs: Cover: Peter Correz/Tony Stone Images; p. 1: (tl) Peter Correz/Tony Stone Images; (tm) Camille Tokerud/Photo Researchers, Inc.; (tr) Paul Barton/The Stock Market; (ml) Charles Gupton/The Stock Market; (mm) Myrleen Ferguson/Photo Edit; (mr) Tony Freeman/Photo Edit; (bl) Penny Gentieu/Tony Stone Images; (bm) Lori Adamski Peek/Tony Stone Images; (br) Ken Fisher/Tony Stone Images; p. 2: Charles Gupton/The Stock Market; p. 3. Lori Adamski Peek/Tony Stone Images; p. 4: Tony Freeman/Photo Edit; p. 5: Camille Tokerud/Photo Researchers, Inc.; p. 6: Myrleen Ferguson/Photo Edit; p. 7: Photodisc, Inc; p. 8: Michael Newman/ Photo Edit; p. 9: Penny Gentieu/Tony Stone Images; p. 10: Paul Barton/The Stock Market; p. 11: Gary Conner/Photo Edit; p. 12: Yellow Dog Productions/Image Bank.

© 1999 by Scholastic Inc.

This edition © 2001 by Scholastic Ltd, Villiers House, Clarendon Avenue, Leamington Spa, Warwickshire CV32 5PR

British Library Cataloguing-in-Publication Data. A catalogue record for this book is available from the British Library.

ISBN 0-439-01935-4

Printed by Lynx Offset Ltd, Chalgrove.

1 2 3 4 5 6 7 8 9 0   1 2 3 4 5 6 7 8 9 0

Do you know how we say hello?

Hola (o-la)

Bonjour (bon-zhoor)

Ciao (chow)

Jambo (jam-bo)

שלום (sha-lome)

你好 (nee-haow)

नमस्ते (na-ma-stay)

Oi (o-ee)

今日は (koh-nee-cheewa)

Aaniin (ahh-neen)

Goodbye!

HELLO!

Saying hello, greeting each other, is one way that people worldwide acknowledge that we are all here together, sharing the earth. And it's a way of reaching out to others to begin to get to know each other, a step towards understanding how we are the same and how we are different.

How do you say hello? The children pictured in *Hello!* represent many cultures and many lands. But every one of them – from the Japanese boy to the Israeli girl – could live in the United Kingdom. It is not unusual now to see classrooms in our cities filled with children from many different cultural backrounds. People move countries for many different reasons. Some because conditions in their own countries are unsafe, others because they hope for a better life, or because they are joining relatives. Europe has always been a place where many languages are spoken and English has many words borrowed from other languages around the world. How many ways can you and your friends say hello?

Celebrating who we are Saying hello in a new language reminds us that each of us is unique: we each have our own special words and ways. Yet every child in *Hello!* is also saying the very same thing! In this book alone, children use 11 different languages to say hello. The Chinese way to say hello, "Ni hao", is the most common: Chinese is spoken by about 1 billion people. But language is not the only way we say hello: we also wave, shake hands, bow, smile and use our bodies, faces and hands to greet each other. Finding a new way to say hello allows us to explore different languages, customs and cultures – and make new friends at the same time!

Where in the world? Languages and those who speak them rarely stay in one place – they circle the globe. So if a child says "Bonjour", he may hail from Canada, France, Louisiana, Martinique or Guyana! Or he might live right next door to you! It's important to remember that when someone has an accent – that is, she sounds different from you – it means that she knows more (not less) than you do. She knows another language! That's why learning to say hello in many ways is so wonderful – it's your ticket to a trip around the world and the friends you have yet to meet. Saying hello is just the beginning of getting to know someone, but what a wonderful start.

Language glossary